THESE
KIDS

Teaching in a Residential Care Setting:
A Survivor's Guide

Allan Sherwood

authorHOUSE®

AuthorHouse™ UK
1663 Liberty Drive
Bloomington, IN 47403 USA
www.authorhouse.co.uk
Phone: 0800.197.4150

© 2018 Allan Sherwood. All rights reserved.

No part of this book may be reproduced, stored in a retrieval system, or transmitted by any means without the written permission of the author.

Published by AuthorHouse 03/28/2018

ISBN: 978-1-5462-8990-6 (sc)
ISBN: 978-1-5462-8989-0 (hc)
ISBN: 978-1-5462-8988-3 (e)

Print information available on the last page.

Any people depicted in stock imagery provided by Getty Images are models, and such images are being used for illustrative purposes only.
Certain stock imagery © Getty Images.

This book is printed on acid-free paper.

Because of the dynamic nature of the Internet, any web addresses or links contained in this book may have changed since publication and may no longer be valid. The views expressed in this work are solely those of the author and do not necessarily reflect the views of the publisher, and the publisher hereby disclaims any responsibility for them.

Dedication

For all those children and young people who, in spite of the odds being stacked against them, manage to make something of their lives.

Introduction

*This is the story of Sammy and how he came to be
famous throughout the world—a real celebrity.*

*Sammy was a dreamer who dreamt both night and day.
Half the time he lived his life in total fantasy.*

*He was not a bad lad, yet not was he good,
In many ways, like all of us, depending on his mood.*

These are the opening lines of a play I wrote in 1989 called *Sammy's Dream*. Sammy lives in a community home with education (CHE). In the play, if you suspend your disbelief, Sammy really does become world famous. He gets adopted by Olga and Yuri Androchev, the first couple in space. He leaves his residential home amid celebrations and hanky waves from tearful peers. Happy ending! Result! *Perestroika* and *Glasnost* abound. The cheeky, cute little kid in care gets a family, and they all live happily ever after.

These Kids is not Sammy's story; it's mine. Sammy's story provides the background for me to reflect on my initial experiences as a teacher in a residential setting for children in public care. The way Sammy, his peers, and the adults are portrayed in the play reflect the reality of the situation as I saw it at the time. As you will discover, I had massive amounts to learn about the care and education of children in public care.

PART 1

THE SEVEN RULES

The Seven Rules

1. Never underestimate the ability of these kids to carry out what they tell you they intend to do.
2. Accept that you will never crack it.
3. Be comfortable in your own skin.
4. Remember that any personal information you divulge will come back to haunt you.
5. Never take their goodwill for granted.
6. Don't fall for the sympathy vote.
7. Don't look for love.

Chapter 1

NOT GETTING IT

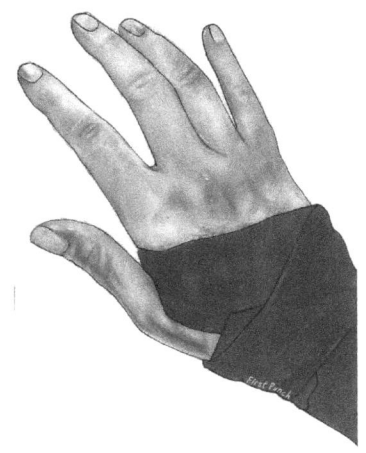

At the interview, held at the rambling pile that was the home of The National Children's Home (NCH) in Congleton, England, I thought I could cope. No problem.

"You know, Mr Sherwood, these children can display some rather bizarre behaviours."

Bizarre? I had just spent three years working in Coalville with punks, goths, and rockers—and that was just the staff! On reflection, I was given fair warning of what to expect. But it's amazing how you can shut out what you don't want to hear. I mean, the advert for a start. It was one of those "subject specialism less important—more an ability to cope with challenging behaviour" type of thing. Why didn't I think through the implications of what the advert could mean? After all, I was hardly a spring chicken. I had already been teaching for fourteen years: two years in East Kilbride teaching speech and drama, five years in Sweden teaching English as a foreign language (TEFL), and seven years in Leicestershire teaching drama with some music thrown in. And all great fun, by the way. I had encountered difficult kids and managed difficult situations. But these kids were the EBDs; that is, those having emotional and behavioural difficulties (the term in vogue at that time). I was soon to discover that they were off the scale in terms of any other kids I had come across. Today, when I am the one interviewing candidates, I find myself wondering, *Does this person have the same mind-set I used to have? Will this person be able to hack it?* Even more than just being able to "hack it", I would pose the questions, *Will this person be effective? Does this person have the potential to interact effectively with these unhappy, damaged young people and be a positive influence on their lives?*

That is the other sad truth about working in residential care. I suppose anyone can hack it for a time—for a few days (on supply), weeks, months, or even years. But I have come to the conclusion that there is a massive distinction between *coping* with a situation and *managing* it.

I would like to think that, for most of the past twenty years, I have been able to manage the behaviour and education of the children in my care. However, if I'm honest—and we must be in this game—there have been days when I have just turned in. On those days, I have coped with whatever the kids have thrown at me, often literally. That's when you have to stand back, put things in perspective, and get on with it.

I did the US summer camps bit in the late seventies and picked up the "keep things in perspective" view from Neal Goldberg, the camp director. Neal used to tell the young counsellors (I was an old boy at twenty-six) that they would have difficult times, but if it was a bad ten minutes, they should see it as ten minutes out of one hour. If an hour, then they should look on it as one out of the twenty-four in the day. If it was a week, well, the summer lasted for three months. I found this distancing technique to be reassuring when chaos ruled in the classroom!

Those of us getting a bit long in the tooth are quick—sometimes too quick—to justify our positions when our effectiveness is called into question. "Who the bloody hell are *they*— Office for Standards in Education, Children's Services and Skills (OFSTED), Care Quality Commission et al.—to criticise *us*! *They* couldn't do it! Let *them* spend a few days here; that'll sort the buggers out! That's all right then. It doesn't matter if my performance isn't up to the mark because they've got sod-all chance of getting anyone else to work with these kids." Well, not really. Recruitment and retention are issues in residential care. Not everyone wants to work in the sector, but it is high-order arrogance to assume no one else could be as effective as you. But back to the NCH and Congleton. If the advert didn't warn me off, a short conversation I had with the principal about temporary accommodation should have left me in no doubt about what I was getting myself into.

The situation was this. It was 1988. My (then) wife and I had just sold up in Leicester and were trying to buy a house in Cheshire. Nightmare! I remember phoning up estate agents, booking a time to view a house, driving north for two hours, and by the time I got there, some other unfortunate like me had bought it without even seeing it. Mrs Thatcher's Britain, eh? So, despairing at the lack of housing as my start date drew nigh, I rang up the principal and asked if I could rent an apartment on the premises to tide us over. He told me he was unable to help and added, "Mr Sherwood [terribly formal], I really don't think that this is the sort of environment to bring your wife and family into." But I still didn't get it. I was just annoyed that he wouldn't help us out.

What is that line from "The Boxer" by Paul Simon? "A man hears what he wants hear and disregards the rest." That was me to a T, and by October, half-term 1988, my situation resembled that of another boxer—Ruben Carter in Bob Dylan's "Hurricane": "Three months later the ghettoes are aflame, Ruben's in South America fighting for his name." The learning curve had begun.

Allan Sherwood

The First Punch

Do you remember those spot-the-difference drawings in the children's section of *The People's Friend*? My old gran used to get it. Or those before-and-after photographs of fat people who became thin. Or wee, pale, skinny guys who morphed into golden-muscled he-men? Well, it was a bit like that for me when the First Punch happened. Ever the eternal optimist, I got over it reasonably quickly. At least I thought I did at the time, and something along the lines of normal service was resumed fairly soon afterwards. But in truth, I was in turmoil. It felt as if my professional life was collapsing about me, and I wondered what the hell I had let myself in for.

However, the First Punch from this kid—let's call him Jonny—marked the beginning of my real learning about the nature of children in public care. It was the point at which I began to develop an understanding of how—and how not—to manage their behaviours.

As I mentioned previously, I had come to work for NCH about two months earlier. Formerly a mainstream drama specialist, I'd had a brilliant time in Leicestershire, taking part in countywide festivals, directing a play for the Edinburgh Fringe, putting on concerts and productions, attending high quality in-service education and training (INSET) with Gavin Bolton, nonetheless—and working jointly with colleagues from other schools. But, as we all know, nothing stays the same, and by age thirty-seven, I was starting to wonder, *Do I really want to be the sad, old guy at the back playing the guitar with kids when I am forty-five?* In fact, the way things panned out for me, I never stopped being—and I still am—the sad old guy in the back, playing guitar, and happy with it. I had also become a dad with the birth of my daughter, and I had become aware of my own mortality and all that. All told, the old energy levels weren't quite what they used to be. I began reflecting on what I wanted from my job and my life. It didn't help when old Ken Baker came on the scene, telling us we had to do 1,265 hours or else! For many of us, that pronouncement was when goodwill flew straight out the window, never to return.

Anyway, back to 1988. I arrived to start work in Cheshire refreshed, up for it, ready for a new challenge, and generally feeling good about myself. The north-west was the ideal location for family reasons, and the job offered the prospect of a better work-life balance than I had previously experienced. So how did it come about that at half-term down the line I found myself lying on the playground having been smacked one?

First of all, I should have given more consideration and attention to the close calls I had experienced up till that point. Like the occasion when I'd come across a kid "kicking off" and started laughing at him; I didn't think he was serious. Yet I'd carried blindly on in Bertie Wooster mode: "Come on now, Carruthers, that's enough. Cut it out. A joke's a joke, old boy, what?" I just didn't appreciate that he was genuinely in a rage—not entirely a helpful sort of response for a chap to give.

Another near miss occurred when I put out my arm to stop a pupil leaving a drama lesson. He really went off on one. Minus the expletives, his response went along the lines of, "Touch me again, and I will hurt you badly!" But instead of heeding the danger signs, I went off on a long spiel about how I hadn't really touched him, and if he hadn't tried to leave, I wouldn't have had to put out my arm in the first place. It's not that what I said wasn't true; it was probably just the wrong time to start a debate about the rights and wrongs of the situation. The issue of touching between teachers and pupils is a massive one and likely to be even more problematic for children in public care. In spite of my lack of understanding, I emerged from this encounter unscathed. However, this was not the case in the following scenario.

I was on afternoon playground duty on a blustery October afternoon. I had done my rounds of the outside toilets, looking for smokers, and come to rest on the edge of the playground watching a few lads kick a ball around. Out of the blue, Jonny boy appeared in front of me. I call it the First Punch incident. The conversation went something like this:

JONNY: I'm going to effing-well hit you.

AL: What?

JONNY: I said I'm going to effing-well hit you.

AL: No, you're not!

(Jonny punches Al. Al falls to tarmac.)

And that was that. Short, not so sweet, but definitely to the point. Now I see it through a glass darkly, but then I saw it face to face. I didn't actually teach Jonny. I found out afterwards that some other lads had put him up to it. (Perhaps the two I mentioned above. Who knows?) It was a setup. Jonny was easily led. They got him to do what he wanted, and I played my part in true thespian tradition. They obviously had me sussed better than I had them.

I can't remember exactly what happened immediately afterwards, but I do recall that, one, the principal had a chat with me (debriefing), and two, a colleague made me a cup of tea (staff care).

Colleagues are always very supportive and understanding in situations like this. They have all been there, or if they haven't they know a man or a woman who has.

So what did I learn from this close encounter? Here I turn to rule one of The Survivor's Guide:

1. **Never underestimate the ability of these kids to carry out what they tell you they intend to do.**

Basic, isn't it? And you would think that an experienced educator would have known better. But I didn't. We all accept that Jonny shouldn't have done what he did—even he accepted that, eventually. But it took me just as long to acknowledge my part in the situation and to accept that I could have done more to prevent it. Jonny told me he was going to hit me, and I told him he wasn't. He must have thought, *Cheeky bastard! Doesn't he realize I'm serious?* And then he sorted me out.

If I had realized that Jonny actually intended to hit me, what could I have done to de-escalate the situation? Would I play it differently now? The short answer is, yes I would.

Nowadays my response could go something like, "John, I know you might want to do that, but do you think that's for the best?" Or, "John, I'm sorry you're upset, but let's talk about it over *there*." And I would indicate the office, staffroom, or somewhere else where there would be other adults around. I don't doubt for one minute that either of these simple responses would have produced a miraculous conversion in Jonny's attitude towards me, but either would have bought me time and served to distract Jonny momentarily from his pre-determined purpose of throwing a punch at me.

What did I do? I ignored the rule to my cost and made no attempt to manage the situation in a professional manner. Of course, Jonny could have hit me anyway, but at least I would have had the satisfaction of knowing that the incident took place despite my best efforts to de-fuse it. I now understand that, in any contretemps that develops or springs up between an adult and a young person, the adult has got to take responsibility for the outcome and take the heat out of the situation. If the young person is giving it laldy (that is bawling and shouting for you non-jocks out there). Then the adult should be talking in measured tones; if the young person is throwing objects around the room, the adult has to remain physically calm.

Another thing I learned from the First Punch was how thin is the veneer of civilization and conformity to accepted traditional, upright values which cover us. I had always considered myself to be a decent, responsible sort of bloke—a pillar of society in my own small way, public servant, et cetera. I remember once, before I worked in this field of education, having a discussion with Tony, a colleague in Leicester, my part of which went along the lines of, "I mean, what kind of society do we live in that locks up kids? Absolutely disgusting, isn't it?" It wasn't that after the First Punch I suddenly wanted to shed my liberal views and join the Blackshirts, but I started to temper my views with a dose of realism. Having worked in local authority secure accommodation and a young offenders' institution, I can see why our society (and, in my view, quite justifiably) locks up children. I broke my own rule with the First Punch incident. I had completely underestimated Jonny's ability to carry out what he told me he was going to do. My education about what it takes to work as a teacher in residential care had begun.

Chapter 2
LEARNING TO COPE

(Scene: Head's office. The head and Sammy are talking.)

THE HEAD: And if your timekeeping doesn't improve, we'll have to make sure you go to bed earlier. And you know what that means …

SAMMY: Yes, sir.

THE HEAD: No going out at night, no special treats.

SAMMY:	No, sir.
THE HEAD:	And we don't want that, do we?
SAMMY:	No, sir.
THE HEAD:	You're not a bad lad, Johnstone, just … well, just …
SAMMY:	I do try sir.
THE HEAD:	I know you do, Johnstone, but you've got t'learn t'be on time!

So, the First Punch incident marked the beginning of my understanding of the make-up of pupils with emotional and behavioural difficulties, as they were then referred to. As I write now, the favoured descriptor is behavioural, emotional, and social difficulties (BESD). Terminology may change, but pupils present the same behaviours—they are aggressive, disaffected, prone to mood swings, and lacking in motivation. When I wrote *Sammy's Dream*, I had a very basic understanding of the needs and nature of pupils with EBD, as the above extract shows. I portrayed Sammy as basically a good kid who just needed a bit of guidance to get him back on track. The reality is that the needs of young people in residential care are complex, and despite everyone's best efforts to support these kids, they many never get their lives back on track. Their lives have often been chaotic from the outset with the absence in childhood of the routine and structure that many of us take for granted. As teenagers, they are still in chaos.

The next scene takes place in the classroom. For what seems the tenth time in the lesson, Suzie has leapt up from the desk, sent paper, pencils, and books crashing to the floor with a sweep of the arm and moves as if to leave the room. You think, *Right, that's it!* You aren't quite sure what you are going to do, but you know you've had enough. You know that Suzie has had a terrible home life, and you have a lot of sympathy for her. Most of the time you feel desperately sorry for her, but not now. Now it's *make-a-stand time*.

Suzie can see that you are working up to something because you are not in your usual genteel come-on-now-let's-calm-down-and-not-be-silly mode. The other kids sense a change in you as well, and they are expectant and bright eyed with excitement about what is about to happen. You get to the door before Suzie does, and the conversation runs something like this:

SUZIE: What do you think you are doing?

You are not quite sure but you settle for:

YOU: I'm blocking the door.

SUZIE: I can see that, you dickhead, so move!

YOU: No.

SUZIE: Get out the bloody way before I bloody well knock you one!

You realize you have got yourself in a spot, but you have gone past the point of no return. You know Suzie pretty well. There is a fifty per cent chance that she will lash out—it's a risk, but based on your knowledge of Suzie, it's a calculated risk. So you say:

YOU: Suzie, I am not going to move, and if you want to leave the room, you are going to have to get past me.

The other kids are going, "Oooh, get him!" They are loving it. This is live soap.

SUZIE: Move!

YOU: No!

If Suzie hits you, it will be no good going to your line manager and bleating on about how horrible Suzie has been to you because you chose to manage the situation in the way you did. You have to go into a situation like this with your eyes open and consider what the outcomes might be for you, for Suzie, and for your organization. Okay, you may have made your stand, but you are not much use to anyone if you then have two weeks off work as the result of an injury.

So, what happens?

First case scenario: Suzie realizes she is out of order and sits down, but not before she makes a comment like, "All right, calm down. I only wanted to go to the toilet." or "You know, you really need some anger management training!" Either comment maintains Suzie's cred in front of her peers. The lesson resumes.

Second case scenario: You get hit (a glancing blow). Suzie leaves the room, and you get back to the lesson.

Third case scenario: You get hit (a nasty one), and you leave the room to get help and some TLC.

Of course, the rights and wrongs of my response to Suzie are open to debate. But is there one correct response? Is it right to challenge unacceptable behaviour in this way? How far do we let kids go before we intervene? Following an incident of this nature, the responses of the other young people present can be a means of learning. In my experience, perhaps surprisingly, I have found that many of the young people I have worked with have a well-developed sense of fair play. If, for example, a comment such as "She was totally out of order there!" is made, you know that, as far as that kid is concerned, you have handled the situation in an appropriate manner. If, on the other hand, the kids are silent or leave to see if Suzie is all right, then you may want to look at your responses and see if you could have handled things in a different way. But no matter how such incidents panned out, as I was beginning to understand, the onus needed to be on me, the adult, to resolve matters. I found this quite hard to accept initially, especially if I felt I was the "injured" party. But the reality was that Suzie would not go away. She wouldn't be excluded or moved on, as has likely to have been her experience in mainstream education. Suzie would be there the next day expecting, quite rightly, to be taught. And although my response and comments to colleagues in the staff room might have been very different, towards Suzie I needed to act responsibly, professionally, and make things right between us.

So, in learning to cope with Suzie and her ilk, I was also coming to understand the second rule of the guide:
2. Accept that you will never crack it.

It took me a long time to fully accept this one. When I was in the States a few years ago, one of the tour guides, as an icebreaker, asked the assembled party for their countries of origin. When he asked, "Anyone here from the UK?", and we duly responded, he said, "Ah, yes, the UK where you have four seasons—*sometimes in one day!*" He was right, of course, and his observation is equally true about children in public care. Their moods can change rapidly in a single day or over short periods of time. This unpredictability in their behaviour can be very disconcerting if you have not been forewarned about it.

Somewhere along the line, probably prior to teacher training college, I had picked up on the fact that, if you show respect to pupils, then the sentiment will be reciprocated. In most cases, certainly in the '70s and '80s, generally speaking, I found this to be the case. A newly qualified teacher or a teacher new to a school can require a bit of time to suss out the lie of the land—with other members of staff as well as the kids. After a period of time, say six months, you know where you stand. Your working relationships will be sorted out with colleagues, and you will know which classes or individual kids you get on with and which you don't. You can steel yourself for Wee Mary in 4R or Big Willie in 1K (affectionately known as "Special K" in East Kilbride). But all these potentially difficult situations are known hazards. You can always rely on Wee Mary to give you a rough time, and Special K kids are a nightmare for even the most experienced of teachers. And, although respect may not always be reciprocated, there is usually enough of it floating around to get you through those times when it is lacking.

Children in public care present a different challenge. Although they deserve the same respect as any other young person, there is no guarantee that the respect will ever be reciprocated. If and when it is, the occasion does not mark a watershed in that particular teacher/pupil relationship, but should be regarded as existing *for that moment only*. Most young people in public care end up there because they have been mistreated by adults. Experience has taught them to be cautious and wary of any adults who befriend them and take an interest in their welfare. Why should teachers expect to be treated any differently?

For some of the young people, there may come a time—perhaps after a year or more—when you feel you are about to crack it. You know this because, when you ask a question, you get an open answer. You respond, and another exchange takes place. It's called a conversation! As I recall, when I first came into this field, some of my initial attempts conversation went something like this:

ME: Going home this weekend?

YP: Might be.

ME: Watch the match last night?

YP: Might have done.

ME: Didn't I see you at the fair on Saturday?

YP: Who wants to know?

I was thinking, *What the hell is wrong with these kids? Can't they see I'm a decent bloke?* But you can't be resentful or act all hurt if the kid doesn't want to talk to you. That's how it is. All in good time—*their* time.

Again, because we are flesh and blood, we get hurt when our good works are thrown back in our faces and the kids don't play the game the way we want it. I remember a residential social worker who took two kids to Blackpool one Sunday. They had a great time—the rides, the beach, McDonald's, ice creams—the lot! When they came back, Bob said to me, "Great trip! The kids were brilliant. And, by the way I've had a word with Tony and Matt. You won't have any trouble with them tonight."

Well, you can guess what happened. Bob was off down the road not more than ten minutes when Tony and Matt started their antics. At the same time, Bob was in the pub saying to colleagues, "You see, it's how you handle them. Take Tony and Matt. Today it was a pleasure—I mean a real *pleasure*—to take those lads out." Meanwhile, Tony and Matt were on the roof swigging some cider they had nicked on the Blackpool trip behind Bob's back. They were waking up other kids by banging on their windows and generally being royal pains in the ass.

The next morning, when Bob came on shift bright eyed and bushy tailed from his eight hours, he was devastated to hear the news that Tony and Matt had kept the site awake for half the night and were now refusing to get up for school. The poor chap was gutted, "How could they? How could they? They promised!" The thing was that Bob thought he had cracked it, but he had been lulled into a sense of false security by the undoubted success of his trip, and he had attached more importance to the outcome than he should have done.

Chapter 3

DEALING WITH PERSONAL COMMENTS

(Scene: The Staffroom. Mr Webb ["Spider"] and Mr Brown ["Golilocks", as he is nearly bald] are addressing some pupils who are milling around.)

MR BROWN: Hey, come on, you two, outside! It's time for break!

BOY: All right, all right. Keep your hair on!

MR BROWN: No need to be cheeky!

MR WEBB: *(Opens the window and shouts.)* Hey you! Get off that roof—now! *(To Mr Webb.)* These kids! These kids!

MR BROWN: Here, do you know what?

MR WEBB: Not till you tell me.

MR BROWN: There I am in the street …

MR WEBB: The street …

MR BROWN: With me girlfriend …

MR WEBB:	Girlfriend, yeh.
MR BROWN:	And up he comes!
MR WEBB:	Who?
MR BROWN:	What's 'is name? Johnstone.
MR WEBB:	Oh, him!
MR BROWN:	Yeh, him. And he says to her—straight out, mind, no messing—he says to her, "Who's this then, yer granddad?"
MR WEBB:	The cheeky monkey. You know it's no wonder me hair's going grey.
MR BROWN:	At least you've got yours!

I'm sure you'll agree that the personal comments directed to Mr Webb and Mr Brown revealed in the above conversation are hardly anything to write home about. Perhaps you even missed them! Reading the dialogue again, I am stuck by how light hearted everything seems. Even the term "cheeky monkey" betrays my lack of understanding of the true nature of many of the young people I have worked with over the years. When I wrote the play, I barely understood why they behaved the way they did; neither did I know how they had come to be in a community home with education on the premises. It was not until I completed my diploma in professional studies in education (DPSE) in special needs (generously sponsored by NCH, thank you) that I at last started to get a handle on what made these kids tick and where they fitted in to the system.

Like Bob, whom I mentioned earlier, we've all been there. For example, I sat in a review meeting and gave a really glowing, honest report about a young person's progress, and as I left for home that night, that same young person was up a tree, refusing to come down, and letting the entire neighbourhood know that I was a wanker of the very highest order. Mind you, if "wanker" is the worst thing you ever get called by these kids in the course of the time you spend with them, then you could argue the point that you had, in fact, cracked it. Because when it comes to dishing out insults, these kids are expert and without comparison. In the parallel *Kids' Survival Guide*, there must be, I feel, a section which reads:

How to insult teachers and carers:

1. *Make a derogatory comment about a prominent physical feature of the person to be insulted.*
2. *Add something negative about the person's nationality.*
3. *Conclude with a swear word.*

Follow this easy formula and you will soon be delivering insults with the best of them. Good luck!

So, if you want to survive long term in this field of work, I would suggest you take a long hard look at yourself in the mirror, inhale deeply, and make an honest assessment. If you are a bit overweight, be prepared for *fat*. Pleasingly slim becomes *skinny* in their eyes. Slightly thinning hair? You're *baldy*. Depending on your other features you will get *big-nosed*, *big eared*, *fat bellied*, and *four-eyed* (if you wear glasses). You may also discover things about yourself that you were hitherto unaware of.

A standard one for me was, skinny, grey-haired, Scottish bastard. (Note that two physical features were skilfully combined for maximum effect.) Sometimes I would get "Irish" instead of "Scottish", in which case I took great delight in saying, "Bastard, maybe, but Irish? No!" Within a week of becoming a manager, I had been elevated to "posh, stuck-up, snobby twat." Interesting that the physical and national elements were missing. Good subject for a dissertation for somebody somewhere no doubt! It was the "posh" tag that really amused me about this one. I have had mixed responses to my Glaswegian accent over the years. Whereas some of my Swedish colleagues confessed they were struggling to understand me, a week later when I was home for the Christmas break, some potential in-laws were asking me, "Where do you come from, pal? You sound a bit effing posh to me!" And I still get it today in Cheshire. You're out for the evening for a nice meal and a few drinks with friends, you go up to the bar place your order, and the bloke standing next to you says, "You've come a long way for a drink!" But I digress.

Returning to dealing with personal comments ... I remember one kid called Shauno. He had been through the physical features, nationality, swear word routine with no response from me. He decided to up the ante by ripping into my family. (There's a lesson to be learned here—see rule 4). It wasn't pleasant to listen to Shauno's graphic, detailed suggestions of what my nearest and dearest was getting up to when I wasn't with her, or what I did to my kids when I was with them. Anyway, I was thinking, *You little shit! Why bring my family into it? What harm have they done to you?* However, from Shauno's point of view, anything associated with me was, as they say, a legitimate target. I could feel the old blood rising, and I was weighing up the possibility of giving him one good hard kick in the knackers and leaving the profession in disgrace. But then I heard him say something about a T-shirt, and he stopped speaking. This distracted me from my reverie. I mumbled a vague, "What?" And he repeated his last phrase which was, "And yer no-name T-shirt!"

So that was it. The final insult. He had saved the worst till last. Failing to get a reaction from conventional forms of insults, Shauno had gone for the non-designer T-shirt that I was wearing for that PE lesson. Needless to say, his comment didn't get the reaction he wanted. I actually laughed at the absurdity of it all, and the tension was defused. The insults that these kids throw at you have one purpose only—to get you to react and lose your cool. They love it! It gives them control and power in circumstances in which they are themselves extremely disempowered. The key to dealing with personal comments is rule number three:

3. Be comfortable in your own skin.

Know who and what you are, and be comfortable with it. Be honest with yourself. Take a step back. Get things in perspective. Stand outside the situation and look in. Listen to the words being said, but see past them. You are the adult in the situation, and you are responsible for managing it.

The young woman who is insulting you has been dealt a poor hand of cards in her life.

She is unhappy and resentful. She is distrustful of adults. She wants to hurt you because she herself has been hurt. Remember too that the reason you are coming in for all this stick is probably because you have crossed her in some way, and she doesn't like it. You may have said, "I'm sorry, Julie, but you are not allowed to go out tonight." And she has gone up one. The fact that Julie, on the previous evening, didn't come in on time, was reported missing, and was eventually returned—drunk—by the police at two in the morning is neither here nor there as far as she is concerned. You are the one who is out of order, not her.

There is always the temptation to give back as good as you are getting, and I don't want to give the impression that I have never made a sarcastic comment to a young person who has insulted me. As I have said elsewhere, we are flesh and blood, and these kids will hold nothing back in their quest to wind us up. They know exactly which buttons to press. Remember, they are experts! I didn't always get it right. When I was new to the field, senior colleagues would tell me, "Don't take it personally." Well, all I would say to that—even now—is that it's hard not to. What does help, though, is realizing that you are doing your job properly. All young people need boundaries, and in my experience, children in public care need them more than most, although boundaries and restrictions on their freedom is what they don't like.

Your lack of a reaction will let a kid know that to try and wind you up by commenting about your appearance or your family or your car or whatever takes their fancy is a non-starter.

If you say, "How dare you talk to a teacher like that?" you are on to a loser straight away and have probably confirmed her already-prejudiced view of teachers as a bunch of stuck-up, snobby twats!

Chapter 4

GETTING THE BALANCE RIGHT

I would argue that, in the potpourri of teacher-pupil relationships, for pupils to learn more about their teachers as *human beings*, including their frailties, is normal, healthy, and generally to be encouraged. In the case of Shauno, whom I mentioned earlier, I hadn't sat him down and said, "Now listen up, laddie, you may see me as the chap who teaches you English, drama, and music, but aren't you amazed to discover that I have a wife and two offspring?" He was aware of my background. In educational settings, information is shared staff to staff, pupil to pupil, staff to pupil, and vice-versa. This is how we function, and I believe learning for all is enriched through this sort of interaction. But when you come to teach in a residential setting, I think you need to be selective about the information you give out, and more guarded in your responses than you may have been previously. When kids in mainstream education glean bits of information about their teachers, it may be shared at home or amongst themselves, but I would be surprised if many consciously store that knowledge as ammunition for possible use at a later date. And this leads directly to the fourth rule of *The Survivor's Guide*:

4. **Remember that any personal information you divulge will come back to haunt you.**

Over the years, my pupils benefitted from good contacts they established with the drama and dance departments of local universities; notably, Manchester Metropolitan University and University College Chester (now Liverpool University).

The projects undertaken by drama and dance students ranged from one-day workshops to single sessions over a period of weeks. The university lecturers and I were in agreement that a visit to the centre prior to commencing the work proper was an essential part of the process. On this visit, the students familiarized themselves with the centre, viewed the space they were to work in, and met staff and young people. I also talked to the students in general terms about the backgrounds of the young people, the type of drama or dance work that I or previous student groups had undertaken with them, and how they should conduct themselves in their dealings with the young people. Some students asked for "dos" and "don'ts" and in the absence of any definites, I gradually moved to paraphrasing rule number four.

The particular case of one student, Jon, who, along with Sue, had opted to do a video project, serves as a reminder of the need for caution when disclosing personal information. The early stages of the project involved a lot of discussion between the two students and pupils in the course. One of them asked Jon if he had ever smoked dope. After a bit of toing and froing, cajoling, and banter, Jon came clean and said that, yes, he had smoked dope. And that was the end of it—for the time being.

Two weeks later, on the day they were due to do their workshop, Sue telephoned me to say that they were going to be late as Jon's car was playing up. We rescheduled for later in the day, and I explained the reason to the pupils. When the session did get going, the matter of the late start was raised by one young person who suggested that the real reason for the delay was that Jon had been stoned the night before. Well, that was that. No matter what Jon said, he was onto a loser. The more he denied it, the more convinced our young people became that Jon had gone over the score with the old Bob Hope the night before, and sadly any chance of productive work, on that day at least, was lost. "Methinks he doth protest too much!" I've done it myself. I remember being in Boots in Leicester with a female friend. I had lost her, and an assistant, seeing me wander around like a fart in a trance, said to me, "Your wife's over there!" When I replied, "Oh, she's not my wife", her raised eyebrows spoke volumes. Sometimes it's better to say nothing.

On another occasion, Jo, a teacher, on appealing for a pupil's cooperation on the grounds that she was shattered and hadn't slept half the night, received the retort, "Don't bring your personal problems in here!" As colleagues, we knew Jo had a possessive and insanely jealous husband, but how did word get out to the pupils? Did Jo herself open up or did a member of staff let something slip? Who knows? Perhaps these kids are just particularly adept at recognizing oppressed, downtrodden, unhappy individuals—they've all been there.

It was always a standard joke at that particular centre where I worked that, if you wanted to know what was going on, you should ask the kids. Sometimes they offered information that we would really rather not have known. I remember being in one residential unit, passing the time of day with the kids, and asking to no one in particular what I thought was the fairly innocuous question, "Is Tom in tonight, then?" "Tom?" croaked Nikki from the far side of the lounge, "No, he won't be in tonight because Lynn is on and they've split up. He's not shagging her any more. He's shagging Liz—that's why they've split up. Dave's covering for him!" All true, it transpired. I rest my case!

I have already drawn attention to the fact that these kids can swear with the best of them, and once you get to know them, they do sometimes accept remonstrations to moderate their language when it gets out of hand, and they will also accept you swearing in a mild form. I don't know about you, but being a bit of a swearer myself, I make the distinction between swearing about something and swearing at individuals. And whereas the kids I have worked will accept it when I use *damn, bloody*, or even *bugger* on occasions—as in "Ya daft bugger, what'd you go and do that for?"—they are very, very intolerant when bad language is used in their presence by people they are not acquainted with.

In the drama studio, three pupils and I were presenting a play as part of the interview process for the position of children's rights and information officer at our centre. I played the role of a residential care worker who was not sympathetic to the kids. I brushed off the fact that I had forgotten one kid's birthday. I told the kids off for smoking when I had been (contrary to centre policy) smoking outside myself, and denied it when the kids challenged me about it. I was an arsehole who shouldn't be working with kids at all. After the play, the kids interviewed each candidate in turn with questions they had prepared earlier.

"How would you feel," asked Sharon of one of the candidates, "if you were that young person and the care worker had forgotten your birthday?"

"Well," said the candidate, "I would have felt pretty *pissed off!*" The candidate didn't actually stress the words in the way I have transcribed them, but she might just as well have done.

In our post interview discussion about the candidates, Sharon was outraged. "I really objected to her saying 'pissed off'. How dare she! Who does she think she is, talking to us like that!"

Needless to say, that candidate didn't get the job.

Chapter 5

ESTABLISHING YOUR RELATIONSHIP

The next rule necessary for survival when working as a teacher in residential care is this:

5. Never take their goodwill for granted.

I say this because I realize now that I must have done *exactly* this when I worked in mainstream education.

Some days your preparation isn't as good as it should be—and we all have those days, don't we? Whether you have been up late watching the election results, the snooker, a big footy match, or are just generally run down as the end of term approaches, you get away with it because the kids are understanding. In fact, if you are working on a major drama/music production, the kids are positively sympathetic! They cut you some slack and make allowances. They are probably as tired as you are. The daily grind of lessons takes second place when you are saving your energy for *Grease*, *Our Day Out*, or *The Prime of Miss Jean Brodie*. In mainstream education, by and large, I found, too, that I could put in place the broad brushstrokes of a lesson without worrying too much about every detail. In drama, for example, on the theme of "the homeless", I could sing them a verse or two of Phil Collins' "Another Day in Paradise", ask them to make a still image, and I'd be off! There is room in education for this sort of planning. It enables pupils to shape their learning, but it does rely heavily on their cooperation and goodwill. I cannot recall once thinking in my mainstream education days, "Now, what will I do if they *don't* respond to this?"

And it wasn't arrogance. I have never been one for throwing any old rubbish at kids and automatically assuming they would do what I said because I was the teacher. I was realistic enough to accept that I wouldn't engage all of the pupils all of the time. That's life. However, lesson planning was almost always done against a background which *assumed* pupil cooperation.

It therefore comes as quite a shock when a kid says, "Look, knobhead, I've told you, I'm not doing any shitty drama lesson. Not now, not next week, not ever!" Knocks the old wind from the sails somewhat! And when this is picked up on by the other pupils in the room who chip in with "Yeh, this is crap. Let's go!" and they leave the room for the third time that lesson, you might just find yourself taking stock of your position.

Not always, but a situation like this could have developed because you had ignored rule number five.

One drama lecturer I liaised with used to tell her students that, if her kids chose to engage with the work on offer, it was a much truer test of the value and relevance of that work. She was right. These kids would never cooperate simply because teacher-pupil convention says they should. If they don't like what's on offer, they vote with their feet.

Detailed planning is crucial for a successful outcome when working with children in public care. You will often hear people say—and I would say it too—that good relationships are the key to successful engagement. But what does this actually mean in practice? What it doesn't mean is throwing unstimulating material at kids in drab surroundings and being too gushy when they complete a piece of work that even they know is way too easy for them. The kids will have you sussed for a fraud before you know it! Some teachers in this setting think that having a good relationship with pupils means chatting to them over cups of coffee and giving them extended breaks because the conversation is interesting. They couldn't be more wrong! You are the teacher; they are the pupils! Your job is to do all the "teachery" things that these kids expect you to do: plan their lessons, mark their work, turn up on time, be organized, have a sense of humour, and treat them fairly. That's what having a good teacher-pupil relationship means when you work in residential care. It's no different, in fact, to any other teacher-pupil relationship in any other setting. You don't even have to like each other. Your job is first and foremost to educate. I remember one girl telling me how much she enjoyed Jo's English lessons. When I asked her why she said, "Because she makes us work hard!"

Almost without exception, by the time you meet them, your young people in public care will have had a disjointed school career in several mainstream schools, pupil referral units, local authority secure units, home tuition service, and in residential schools, both private and public. Add to this a chaotic home background in a deprived social setting characterized by neglect and abuse and you will start to wonder how they have managed to learn anything at all. As a teacher in residential care, your role is to build on whatever learning they have already gained and help them make progress. Don't try and be their mate; they won't thank you for it and may even resent it!

Chapter 6

BEING FIRM

In much the same way that Bob, whom I mentioned earlier, was upset when Tony and Matt had not come through with the goods after the Blackpool trip, I remember feeling similarly disillusioned after a trip out with pupils to see *Grease* in Manchester. I wouldn't let anything spoil the afternoon—the fact that I had stove in the roof of the minibus on the roof of a multi-storey car park (the kids didn't know because it was dark when we came out), or the fact that young Thomo, on emerging from the stalls at the interval, had necked a half pint of lager set out for another theatregoer. On the return journey, however, sixteen-year-old Julie, suddenly pitched in with, "Have you noticed how Allan is driving faster now because he wants to get home to his wife and kiddies?"

I thought, *What is that all about? Where did that come from?* We'd all had a great time. The trip had gone famously, so why spoil the party? I just couldn't get my head round it.

Over the years, colleagues have confirmed that this type of scenario is not untypical. What seems to be happening is that, yes, the kids in question have had a great time out enjoying each other's and the adults' company, but as they return "home", the reality of their situation hits them, and everything feels like a bit of a sham. When it comes down to it, you have to accept that, however nice you are to them, the young people in care who you are working with would rather be someplace else. Was it thoughts like these that Julie was experiencing as we approached the centre that for the time being was "home" to her? Perhaps the afternoon reminded her of what life could be like or had been like for her in the past. Her way of coping was to sabotage the general feeling of well-being. Her message was, "Okay, so we've had our little cocoon of normality, and now it's back to reality, and in case you've forgotten, take that!"

And in this connection, it is timely to introduce rule number six:

6. Don't fall for the sympathy vote.

Just as these kids are experts when it comes to delivering insults, they are equally adept at producing statements designed to tug at the old heart strings. Don't get me wrong—these kids need and deserve all the support and empathy they can get. But not unconditionally. And certainly not when they have created merry hell all day, marauding round the place; wielding half bricks; brandishing bits of tree; threatening each other, staff, and any other unfortunate punter who crosses their path. However, that is the time when you can guarantee they will pluck statements from the air designed to throw you off balance, shuffle your feet, go misty eyed, and start reaching for the Kleenex. So, if you want to survive, be on your guard!

A classic one is, "And, anyway, you're only doing this job because you get paid for it!"

The first time I heard this one in the early nineties, I didn't go as far as thinking, *She's right. How selfish am I, doing this job for money?* But it did plant a seed of doubt, which I'm sure was the intention. Once you think about the statement and the context, you begin to see that it says more about the kid than it does about you. These kids will have experienced rejection in large doses from the significant adults in their lives. We know it, and they know we know it. So when, in a professional capacity, you respond to the request "Can I go to town with Mel?" and you respond with a firm no because the last time Mel and your fourteen-year-old charge went to town they got drunk and frightened the locals, you will come for some stick. You may be threatened or pushed around a bit and told that you don't care about kids and that you are only in it for the money.

So how do you handle this one? Well, you need to remember that you are getting all this stick because you said no. Pull out a packet of Rizlas and a bottle of cider and say, "Only joking, flower. 'Course you can go out, and here … have these on me!" You would be Mr Wonderful in her eyes (albeit a very-soon-to-be-unemployed one). The "in it for the money" questions your professionalism. You've got to keep your dignity and hold firm.

Another oft-heard quip along the same lines is pulled out of the bag in the calm after the storm when mayhem has been high on the agenda and you are talking through the events with the young people who have been involved. Here is a debrief, 1992 version:

YOUNG PERSON: *(Interrupting you in full flow as you drone on.)* Now just shut up a minute!

YOU: *(Surprised)* Sorry?

YP: It's all right for you saying we shouldn't run off and we should control ourselves and all that, but at the end of the day …

YOU: Yes?

YP: At the end of the day, *you* can get in your car and go *home*, away from *here* and have a break. *You don't live here.* You don't know what it's like. *We do!*

YOU: I suppose you've got a point.

And as they say in Glasgow, "That's you told!"

The kid has made a fair point. I have never been in public care, so I don't know what it feels like to be brought up by adults who are not my birth parents. However, I have spent more than half of my working life educating children in public care. I do have an understanding of their backgrounds, their needs, and what must happen if they are to mature and survive into adulthood. (And, sadly, I have known some young people who have not survived.)

Or does, "You don't live here," mean that, if I had been in care myself as a child, then I would have more cred with the young people in *my* care? Given my knowledge of how these kids operate, I doubt it! I used to accept "You don't live here" as the point where I conceded. Nowadays, depending on the context, the debrief script might run something like this:

YP: It's all right for you! You can go home and have a break, you—

YOU: *(You know what's coming so you interrupt.)* Oh, come on, not that old chestnut!

YP: You can go home—

YOU: Yeh, I know I can go home. And I know you would rather not be here. You'd rather be someplace else. But are you saying that, because I don't live here, I'm not allowed to have opinions about what you do and don't do?

YP: Stop winding me up!

YOU: Am I supposed to let you do what you want and not care about it?

You might consider this to be a bit messy and not necessarily politically correct. Children in public care have often reminded me that they have "a voice". Where do they learn that I wonder? But don't all members of a community have a right to be listened to? I think so. "You don't live here" in contexts like this have often seemed to me to be an attempt to deny adults that right on somewhat spurious grounds.

Chapter 7

LEARNING ABOUT COLLEAGUES

Anyway, returning to Sammy and his chums. What else does the fiction I created tell me about how I viewed things at the time? Let's take a look at the teachers.

MR WEBB: I've had enough!

MR BROWN: Me too.

MR WEBB: I can't go on.

MR BROWN: Neither can I.

MR WEBB: I'm in a big long tunnel, and I can't see the light at the end.

MR BROWN: No light!

MR WEBB: What I need is a holiday.

MR BROWN: A holiday!

MR WEBB: It's weeks till half-term.

MR BROWN: I won't last that long!

MR WEBB: Kids!

MR BROWN: Who needs them?

MR WEBB: A holiday … you don't suppose we could … No. No, we couldn't.

MR BROWN: What are you thinking?

No prizes for guessing what "Spider Webb" is up to. He plans to throw a sickey and slink off for an invigorating couple of days in the fresh air of Wales. Spider convinces the reluctant Mr Brown ("Goldilocks" to the boys—he is completely bald) to join him in the jaunt, and they go off to pack their bags. However, unknown to them, their entire conversation has been overheard by young Sammy, who decides to follow them.

I intended these two characters to be funny and a joke. They just can't hack it any more. They come from an age when kids were taught to be grateful for what they had. Spider and Goldilocks are burnt out and spent up. They would rather be anywhere else than in the classroom teaching *these kids*, not unlike some teachers you and I know who are approaching retirement—except these guys are in their thirties! And were they true reflections of myself and the teaching colleagues I knew at that time? The answer is no, but they do reflect *a type*. This type, I hasten to add, may not restricted to residential care settings. All teachers—even motivated, highly enthusiastic teachers—can get down at times when the pressure for whatever reason gets too much. But *the type* I am alluding to here is the teacher who ends up like our two laddos above because they have become trapped for professional or financial reasons.

I sometimes thought working as a teacher in residential care was like National Service—you did it out of a sense of duty or because you had to. You do your two years and then move on. But what happens if you can't?

Some teachers I knew initially made a conscious decision to work in residential care and then realized, too late, that it wasn't for them and that there was nowhere else for them to go. Compared to their colleagues in mainstream education, they had become de-skilled in their specialisms and were no longer viable on the open market. When I worked in residential care, all teaching posts carried an additional allowance which equated to a promoted post in mainstream education, and this was a further disincentive for some people to move on. Any effective team needs to have balance with regard to gender, age, and experience, and I would add to this a balance in tenure of post. You need experienced people who know the system, but to keep institutions alive—and residential care settings are *institutions* whether we like the word or not—you need innovative ideas, fresh input, and energy that only new staff can bring. You may have heard of the Healthy Schools Programme. Well, how about, particularly for residential care settings, a Healthy Turnover of Staff Program.

When candidates who are new to residential care come for an interview, the message we should give them is this: We will appoint you for the skills you have. If you are appointed, look on your appointment as part of your professional development. Give us one, two, three years—however long you feel you can be effective—and then move on to pastures new.

Working in residential care is not a life sentence, but for some teachers it may become just that with disastrous consequences for themselves and the young people they teach and care for.

Many of the young people we are talking about here have been subject to abuse—physical, emotional, and sexual. They know the care system inside out. They have been moved from one placement to another, settling, often briefly, before their own actions or the wishes of the professionals involved in their care deem another placement to be more suitable. These kids are at the bottom of the pile in terms of opportunity and at the top of the triangle in terms of need. They are simultaneously complex and simple individuals who both crave and reject affection. On the one hand, they resist the attempts of others to establish pattern and order in their lives as an imposition, yet on the other hand, order, structure, and routine are exactly what they need.

There should be enormous flashing signs outside children's homes with the message, "We Never Close"—because they don't! No matter what time you pass by them—morning, noon, the wee small hours, whether you're going to the match or have been to the pub, on bank holidays, Christmas Day, whenever—residential life grinds inexorably on. These complicated, frustrating, angry, unhappy young people present extremes of behaviour which are difficult for themselves and others to manage. The cost of their care and education for a month could pay university tuition fees for a year. And although this may seem scandalous to some, the real scandal is that, until the arrival of national minimum standards (NMS) and the introduction of National Vocational Qualifications (NVQs) in health and social care for staff, virtually *anyone* could become a residential care worker (subject to normal Criminal Records Bureau [CRB] checks, now called Disclosure and Barring Service [DBS] checks). Just consider this for a moment: the care of some of the most damaged young people in society has been trusted to a hotchpotch of individuals with little or no training in the field.

Some residential care workers who came to the role after retirement from jobs which had no relation to the caring profession often proved extremely effective, and the lives of young people would have been all the poorer without their intervention. However, those workers who drifted in because they had a mate, partner, or sibling already in post were often less effective. The problem with this "I'll-sort-you-out-with-a-few-shifts-mate" over a few drinks in the pub approach to recruitment was that it fostered the notion that anyone could do it. And six months into their posts, some of these new recruits present themselves as "experts" at planning meetings and reviews and delivering that infamous line, "Well, he's not a problem for me!" Give me strength! If I had a tenner for every time I have heard that line, you would have been reading *These Kids* years ago due to my early retirement to take up writing full time.

I heard it just the other day, and again I could not believe it. There we all were—social worker, care manager, parent, education manager (yours truly), young person, and keyworker—assembled in the lounge for the planning meeting. We all chipped in our respective bits (with the exception of the keyworker, who was strangely silent at this point), identifying problems and offering praise and encouragement when possible. There was no getting away from it, this kid was having massive problems—violent assaults on staff members and young people and extensive criminal damage, all tied in to his use of cannabis. These facts even the kid acknowledged. When the recently recruited, new-to- the-field keyworker did pipe up it was only to say, "Well, as far as I'm concerned, James is a lovely lad—polite, smashing, and not a problem for me!"

Lord God Almighty! The boy's own mother was afraid of him! How must she have felt hearing that comment! And so it came to pass that this emotive phrase passed into the annals of our staffroom and became standard banter.

If someone said, "You know what? I've just had a really shit lesson with Kaz", the phrase "She's not a problem for me!" would ring out, simultaneously ridiculing people like the "expert" keyworker while offering support to the colleague.

As I have mentioned earlier regarding teachers who work in this setting, anyone can *do* it, but everyone is not equally effective, and it's no different for care staff. These kids suss out early who's who and what's what in the makeup of the staff team. They know those members of staff they can manipulate and those members with whom the buck stops. The sibling-spouse-mate approach to recruitment creates additional problems that the service could do without, and it's easy to see why.

Scenario: You and your partner work as care workers in the same centre. Your loved one comes home with a black eye. There has been an incident. Your partner has been involved in a physical intervention with Cheryl and was assaulted by her. You are Cheryl's keyworker. The next day you are due to take Cheryl clothes shopping, an activity which is long overdue.

Which do you do?

- Take the hump with Cheryl because she has hit your partner and call in sick for the next shift. (Very unprofessional.)

- Go into work the next day and tell Cheryl what you think of her for hitting your partner and because of this you are not going to take her shopping. (Also unprofessional.)
- Take Cheryl on the shopping trip as planned. (This is called "doing your job.")

Footnote: During the shopping trip, Cheryl tells you that the reason she hit your partner was because she called her "a little bitch". When you check this out with your partner, she tells you that she did say that. You know that your partner was clearly out of order and could be suspended pending an investigation.

Difficult one, isn't it?

Chapter 8

LEARNING ABOUT YOURSELF

You don't half learn a lot about yourself when working with these kids.

I return to the conversation I had in 1981 when I had newly returned from Sweden and was enjoying working as a mainstream education drama specialist in Leceistershire:-

TONY: I mean, what kind of society do we live in that locks up kids?

ME: Absolutely, I agree. A real bummer man—awful!

Of course, this short extract from a lengthier conversation on the rights of young people and their roles in society was pre Sammy. Once you've spent a few weeks working in a secure unit, you will begin to understand why it is sometimes necessary to lock up children. Of course, the debate still continues as to whether or not it does the kids any good. The opinions of young people I worked with were split—some detested the whole experience and the system that brought them there; others accepted their "time" as respite and a place of safety from the dangerous circumstances of prostitution, self-harm, and drug dependency, in which they had found themselves embroiled on the "outside". However, the trendy leftie, as I saw myself in 1981, thought it was a disgrace that we lived in a country where children and young people could be deprived of their freedom. Ten years later, I had learned that young people could be locked up for basically one of two reasons: To protect others, and to protect themselves And, furthermore, I accepted this as fair and just. Of course, when considered objectively, it is a terrible indictment on our society that this sad state of affairs exists. However, when it's your car that has been stolen and torched, your house that has been burgled, your property that has been stolen, or your child who has been assaulted, well, people's attitudes change. Through working with these kids, I learned that I was not as liberally minded as I had first thought. And if you, in the course of your career as a teacher, carer, or social worker in residential care, are the one who gets assaulted and verbally abused, I can guarantee that your ability for compassion and turning the other cheek will be tested even further.

> I was devastated by the First Punch. I had been wronged and assaulted. I was a nice guy. I didn't deserve that kind of treatment. I wanted payback. Some colleagues told me I should have the kid charged with assault. I didn't in that particular case, and I should add that over the twenty plus years I worked in residential care, I can recall only two or three occasions when I did such a thing. The reality is that, if you do opt to press charges on a young person for, say, an assault on the Monday, Tuesday morning will see that same young person back in your class with normal service resumed. And that's the way it should be. Another factor which tempers your capacity for revenge or "justice being seen to be done" is that you may be criminalizing the young

person in your care. Again, is this in the young person's best interests? No easy answers, but that is the nature of the work with these damaged and distressed young people.

The last rule of *The Survivor's Guide* is:

7. Don't look for love.

You know, I had no idea how important it was for me as a teacher to be "liked" till I went to work with these kids. It was something I hadn't thought about. If you had asked me when I was a mainstream education drama teacher in Leicestershire if being popular with pupils was important to me, I would have denied it straight away. But the truth was, it was—*massively* important to me. But I didn't realize it at the time! Don't get me wrong, I didn't get on with every single pupil I taught. What teacher does? But the point is that, in mainstream education, through all the disagreements about behaviour or poor work attitude, through all the detentions, the pupils:

- Did their homework
- Came to music and drama club
- Bought teachers presents
- Said thank you when taken on trips
- Offered teachers sweets at break time

I knew I was liked, and that kept me going and feeling good about myself.

So when I went to work in residential care, it took me several months to work out what was missing. There was certainly not, for a long time, any indicators from pupils that let me know where I stood with them, and the worst—the very worst—thing I could have said was: "After what I've done for you …" (referring to an earlier time when I had treated them especially well.)

This would have done me no favours whatsoever and, in my experience, lessened my standing with them. However, when kids in residential care realize you are there for the long haul and that, in spite of their personal insults, abusive comments, and two-fingered gestures towards you and all you stand for, you are still turning up for work every day, you will start to feel their respect and a change in their attitude towards you.

Initially, I found it really hard to understand why, for example, my friendly attitude towards pupils was never reciprocated and was often viewed with suspicion. But as my understanding of these pupils grew and I learned about the nature of their problems and why they behaved the way they did (almost always because of the way other adults had treated them), I found I was able to accept and manage their behaviour much better.

To call myself a "survivor" is a bit tongue in cheek, although when things "kicked off" in the residential home in the aftermath, it did feel like that at times. As to the young people I came across, well Sammys—naughty kids with hearts of gold—they were not. It took me quite some time to realize that when, in the play, the head says to Sammy, "You're not a bad lad, Johnstone, just … well, just …" this reflected my own naïve understanding of the backgrounds of young people who found themselves in residential care—an understanding that I hope to have shown you was flawed.

PART 2

SAMMY'S DREAM

Sammy's Dream

Characters

Sammy Johnstone

Walter

The head—Old Whatisname

Mr Brown—Goldilocks

Mr Webb—Spider

Olga Androchev

Yuri Androchev

The Press of the World

Newscaster

Community service volunteer

Boys

Additional staff as required

Allan Sherwood

Opening Song

(The whole cast sings)

                    This is the story of Sammy
                    and how he came to be
                    famous throughout the world—
                    a real celebrity.

                    Sammy was a dreamer
                    who dreamt by night and day.
                    Half the time he lived his life
                    in total fantasy.

                    He was not a bad lad,
                    yet he was not good.
                    In many ways like all of us,
                    depending on his mood.

                    Sammy's best mate, Walter,
                    thought of him no end.
                    But even he would tell you Sammy
                    drove him round the bend.

WALTER: One day he thinks he's Rambo
                    the next he's Superman,
                    Billy the Kid, or Hannibal
                    or even Ghengis Khan.

                    Now let us ask his teachers
                    for their view of him,
                    What do you think of Sammy Johnstone?

TEACHERS:	He does our heads in.
TEACHER 1:	It's not that he is mental.
TEACHER 2:	It's not that he is mad.
TEACHER 1:	But somewhere there's a screw loose.
TEACHER 2:	It's really very sad.

> In all these flights of fancy
> no matter who he was
> Sammy was the hero
> who always won the cause.
>
> Look at Sammy dreaming now,
> a smile upon his face.
> He dreams he's meeting astronauts
> returning home from space.

(Laughter from teachers and Walter.)

> Now you might think he's bonkers,
> you might think he's cracked,
> but this dream turned out to be
> the real thing—in fact.

(Lights dim. We hear music—low, throbbing, pulsating, becoming a drone. A space capsule is revealed. The door opens, and an astronaut appears. Sammy approaches the astronaut, Yuri Androchev, and shakes his hand. Another astronaut appears: Olga Androchev. Sammy shakes her hand. The Press of the World enter and take photographs. Sammy is crowned King of the World and given a sceptre and crown. The music cuts into the sound of an alarm clock.)

Scene 1

(The dormitory. Sammy is in bed being awakened by the community service volunteer [CSV]).

CSV: Come on, Sammy lad, wake up!

SAMMY: Leave me alone. Go away!

CSV: But, Sam, you'll be late for assembly. You don't want to be gettin' into trouble again.

SAMMY: Oh, ah! Oh, ah! Don't worry, don't worry. *(Getting up.)* Is me breakfast ready? You know, I had this dream. Astronauts!

CSV: Oh yeah?

SAMMY: Yeah, I was talking to them. It was cool, it was great—

CSV: Come on—

SAMMY: I was King of the World! It was boss!

CSV: Not those socks, Sam.

SAMMY: Everyone got to know about Sammy Johnstone. I had me photographs taken with them—

CSV: Get a move on, lad, will you?

(Sam sees a lad go by.)

SAMMY: Hey, you!

LAD:	Yeah?
SAMMY:	Where's that Mars bar you owe me?
LAD:	Mars Bar?
SAMMY:	Yeah. You know you said you'd give me one. You promised, y' promised! *(Aside to the lad)* You know … f' the cig.
LAD:	Oh, ah! Tomorrow, okay?
CSV:	What's all this about?
LAD:	Nothing.
SAMMY:	*(To lad.)* Come on. We'll be late for assembly.

(They start to run off.)

CSV:	And remember to … *(They have gone.)* … clean yer teeth. Oh, I don't know. Why me, why me, eh?

Scene 2

(The Playground. Kids running, jumping, fighting, smoking, playing football. Bell rings.)

Scene 3

(Assembly. We hear the song "All Things Bright and Beautiful". Boys seated in rows. The boys are by no means beautiful. A scruffy lot, they shuffle, look round, pick noses, chew, smirk at the head when he is not looking directly at

them. *Sammy and the lad sneak in at the back. All heads turn. They are not surprised to see Sammy. He is often late.)*

HEAD: Thank you, Mr Jones. *(Music stops.)*

HEAD: *(To the lad.)* I'll see you later. *(To Sammy.)* Johnstone!

SAMMY: Sir?

HEAD: Come here, lad!

SAMMY: But it wasn't just me, sir!

HEAD: Do as you're told, laddie! *(Sammy comes out.)* What time did you wake up today?

SAMMY: *(Whispering.)* Seven o'clock, sir.

HEAD: Speak up, lad!

SAMMY: *(Shouts.)* Seven o'clock sir!

HEAD: And what time is it now?

SAMMY: I don't know, sir. You see, I haven't got a watch.

HEAD: Can you explain why it takes you so long to get here when everyone else can make it on time?

SAMMY: I can, sir!

HEAD: Well?

SAMMY: I fell back to sleep, sir, and I had this dream. I met these astronauts—

HEAD: Spare me the details, Johnstone. Come to my room at four o'clock. Mr Jones?

(Music starts again: "All Things Bright and Beautiful". Song ends.)

HEAD: Now, can anyone tell me what year this is? What *year* this is? *(Hands go up.)*

HEAD: *(Selecting a boy.)* Yes?

BOY: Nineteen eighty-nine, sir.

HEAD: (Irritated.) Yes … yes. But what's special about nineteen eighty-nine?

BOY: Nottingham Forest are in two cup finals, sir.

HEAD: Eh? Yes … but … but … can anyone tell what I'm thinking? What's in my mind?

(Stunned silence from the boys.)

HEAD: *(Exasperated)* Well, come on, where do we live?

(Hands go up.)

BOY: Here, sir!

HEAD: Yes, but where's here?

BOY: The Children's Home, sir.

HEAD: Good, very good. Now, what is special about our home this year?

(Silence and blank faces.)

HEAD: *(Trying a new tack.)* What do all of you have every year? *(Hands go up.)* Yes?

BOY: A new uniform.

HEAD: No. Well, yes, but no … not uniform. Roberts! Come out here!

(Roberts goes out.)

HEAD: Now, Roberts, how old are you?

Roberts: Eh … eh … twelve, sir.

HEAD: And how old were you last year?

Roberts: Eh … (Counting on his fingers.) Nine, ten, *eleven*, sir.

HEAD: *(To the boys.)* Now … what did Roberts have to have in order to make him twelve?

(Hands go up.)

BOY: A birthday, sir.

HEAD: Say that again please.

BOY: A birthday, sir.

HEAD: Yes! And whereas Roberts here is one year older and twelve, our organization is ….much older. Can anyone tell me how old?

(Hands go up.)

BOY: A hundred.

HEAD: No. More than that.

BOY: Five hundred.

HEAD: No. Let's not get carried away. Less than that.

BOY: Three hundred and sixty-five.

HEAD: No. That's the days in the year. Come on now, a hundred and …

BOY: Eighty! *(Imitating a darts commentator.)* A hundred and eighty!

(Laughter from the boys.)

HEAD: Right! That's enough! This year is the one hundred and twentieth anniversary, or birthday if you like, of our organization, and there are a number of special events arranged to celebrate. And if any of you have any ideas to put us in the public eye, then you can come and see me or tell your teachers or care staff. Right? And now a prayer. *(Heads bow.)* Dear God, help us in our weakness and give us the strength we need to face the trials and testing situations that we face in our daily lives. Amen

Allan Sherwood

(All exit to "All Things Bright and Beautiful".)

Scene 4

(The staffroom. Mr Webb and Mr Brown are having tea while the boys mess around at the door.)

MR BROWN: Hey, come on, you lot. Outside! It's time for break.

BOY: *(To Mr Brown, who is nearly bald.)* All right, all right keep your hair on!

MR BROWN: No need to be cheeky!

MR WEBB: *(Opening a window and shouting.)* Hey, you! Get off that roof. Now! *(Closes the window and sits.)* These kids. These kids.

MR BROWN: Don't know why we bother.

MR WEBB: It's a liberty—a blooming liberty.

MR BROWN: If I say one thing …

MR WEBB: They do the other … …

MR BROWN: And if I say the other …

MR WEBB: Don't tell me! *(Pauses.)* Look at my hair …

MR BROWN: I've lost all mine.

MR WEBB: Five years ago, it was black as coal, and now look at it. Chalk white. Pure as the driven snow.

MR BROWN: Unlike them.

MR WEBB: Eh?

MR BROWN: The boys. You can't say that about them.

MR WEBB: What?

MR BROWN: That they're pure as the driven snow.

MR WEBB: That's what I'm saying.

(Pause.)

MR BROWN: You can't trust them.

MR WEBB: You can't! I put down my sandwiches.

MR BROWN: You put down your sandwiches.

MR WEBB: I put down my sandwiches and turn my back …

MR BROWN: And?

MR WEBB: In the bin!

MR BROWN: The bin?

MR WEBB: The bin. They hid them in the bin. It's unbelievable really.

MR BROWN: Here, do you know what?

MR WEBB: Not till you tell me.

MR BROWN: There I am in the street …

MR WEBB: The street …

MR BROWN: With me girlfriend …

MR WEBB: Girlfriend, yeah …

MR BROWN: And up he comes.

MR WEBB: Who?

MR BROWN: What's his name? Johnstone.

MR WEBB: Oh, him!

MR BROWN: Yeah him And he says to her—straight out, mind, no messing—he says to her, "Who's this, then, yer grandad?"

MR WEBB: The cheeky monkey. It's no wonder my hair's gone grey.

MR BROWN: At least you've got yours.

(Bell rings. They get up.)

MR WEBB: Deep breath!

MR BROWN: Here we go!

(As they leave the staffroom, they start to bellow instructions at the boys. They exit.)

Scene 5

(The Head's office. The Head is talking.)

HEAD: … and if your timekeeping doesn't improve we'll have to make sure you go to bed earlier, and you know what that means.

SAMMY: Yes, sir.

HEAD: No going out at night. No special treats.

SAMMY: No, sir.

HEAD: And we don't want that, do we?

SAMMY: No, sir.

HEAD: You're not a bad lad, Johnstone, just … well, just …

SAMMY: I do try, sir.

HEAD: I know you do, Johnstone. *(With emphasis.)* But you've got to learn to be … on time! Now off you go! *(Sammy doesn't move.)* Well, run along then! *(Sammy doesn't budge.)* What's the matter, laddie? Speak up if you've something to say!

SAMMY: Well, sir, it's about what you said in assembly about this being a special year 'n that. I've had an idea.

HEAD: Splendid! Well, what is it? A sponsored walk? A charity football match?

SAMMY: No, sir, I was thinking that if some of us could get on the telly, then everyone—the whole world even—would get to know about us.

HEAD: And how do you suppose we're going to get on the television?

SAMMY: Ah! You'll like this bit, sir. You see, I had this dream. You know when them astronauts come back to Earth in them little capsules?

HEAD: Astronauts, Johnstone?

SAMMY: Yes, sir, astronauts. They come sailing down in the capsule with a little parachute. Haven't you seen it, sir? It's boss!

HEAD: Boss?

SAMMY: Brilliant, sir, really cool. It goes splash in the water, sir. That was me dream y'see, and that's what gave me the idea.

HEAD: The idea being?

SAMMY: Well, I thought the next time some astronauts go into space we could meet them when they come back and then we'd be in the papers and on the telly.

HEAD: Johnstone! I know you have a fertile imagination, but that's the most ridiculous idea I've heard from you in a long time. *(Showing him the door.)* Out you go!

SAMMY: But, sir—

HEAD: No "buts", Johnstone. Out! I'm a busy man!

(Sammy exits.)

Scene 6

(The dorm. Walter is playing with a football. Sammy enters in a bad mood.)

WALTER: Well?

SAMMY: Well what?

WALTER: Are you grounded?

SAMMY: No.

WALTER: Well, what's up wi' you? It looks like somebody's stolen yer last sweetie.

SAMMY: It's him. He won't listen.

WALTER: Who? Old Whatisname?

SAMMY: I've got this great idea, and he won't listen.

WALTER: Well tell us then.

SAMMY: Right. I will. I had this dream, see—

WALTER: Here we go!

SAMMY: Look, I'm serious. In this dream, I was having me photograph taken with these astronauts who'd just come back from space. And then I thought if one of us could do that, we'd be world famous, wouldn't we?

WALTER: Yeah, we would … I s'pose.

SAMMY: What do you think then?

WALTER: It's … different, but it couldn't happen.

SAMMY: Why not?

WALTER: Well, for a kick-off, we don't know any astronauts, and if we did, how would we … oh I'd forget it, Sam. *(An idea comes to him.)* Why not organize a sponsored walk or, even better, a footy match? I'll help you.

SAMMY: That's what he said. You know what's wrong with this place? No one's got any imagination. I'm sick of the lot of you!

(Towards the end of the scene, kids enter and take up positions round Sammy and Walter. Sammy turns away from Walter and faces the audience.)

Song: "The Trouble with Sammy"

(The Kids sing.)

> The trouble with Sammy
> is he won't accept
> that some things can't be done,
> and if you try to
> explain why
> he'll tell you you're spoiling his fun.
>
> Being the hero
> and scoring a goal
> in the final of the FA Cup
> is all very well
> when you are small,
> but not when you're grown up.

(Sammy, Walter, and the kids exit.)

Scene 7

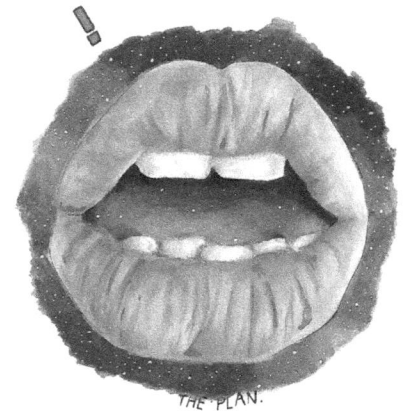

(The staffroom. Sammy sits outside the window. A bell rings. Mr Brown and Mr Webb enter. They do not see Sammy. They open the window.)

MR WEBB: I've had enough.

MR BROWN: Me too!

MR WEBB: I can't go on.

MR BROWN: Neither can I.

MR WEBB: I'm in a big long tunnel, and I can't see the light at the end.

MR BROWN: No light … no light!

MR WEBB: What I need is a holiday.

MR BROWN: A holiday …

MR WEBB: It's weeks till half-term.

MR BROWN:	I won't last that long.
MR WEBB:	These kids!
MR BROWN:	Who needs 'em!
MR WEBB:	A holiday … a holiday. You don't suppose we could … No. No, we couldn't.
MR BROWN:	What are you thinking?
MR WEBB:	No, no. It's … unprofessional.
MR BROWN:	Unprofessional?
MR WEBB:	It's not done. We couldn't. Could we?
MR BROWN:	Do what, for goodness sake?
MR WEBB:	*(He furtively moves to the staffroom door, checks there is no one around and returns to Mr Brown.)* Do I look ill?
MR BROWN:	What?
MR WEBB:	A bit off colour perhaps?
MR BROWN:	Eh?
MR WEBB:	Dark patches under the eyes?
MR BROWN:	I don't get it.
MR WEBB:	You dimwit. There's nothing wrong with me.

MR BROWN: Isn't there?

MR WEBB: No … but there could be. Get my drift?

MR BROWN: *(Loudly.)* Ah! You mean pretend to be ill!

(Sammy pricks up his ears.)

MR WEBB: Not so loud, you idiot!

MR BROWN: *(Whispering.)* Pretend to be sick and have a few days off.

MR WEBB: Why not?

MR BROWN: It's not right. It's dishonest. It's against everything I believe in.

MR WEBB: Look, I know this lovely little spot in Wales overlooking Cardigan Bay. Cliffs, sea breezes, nine-hole golf course.

MR BROWN: Bar?

MR WEBB: They do a lovely pint of real ale in the snug.

MR BROWN: It's a deal. Count me in. *(They shake hands.)* When do we go?

MR WEBB: In a couple of days. So listen, start dropping a few hints today. Come over dizzy, develop a headache or something.

MR BROWN: Dry throat, pains behind the eyes?

MR WEBB: Perfect.

MR BROWN:	Wait a minute. Won't it seem suspicious both of us being off at the same time?
MR WEBB:	Why should it? We're a small community. Remember that time when Old Smiddy broke out in a rash? Within days half the school came down with it. There's nothing to worry about. No one will suspect a thing. *(A bell rings.)* Come on, let's crack on!
MR BROWN:	*(Whistling.)* I feel better already.
MR WEBB:	Well don't … remember?
MR BROWN:	Oh, yeah. *(He coughs.)* Dear, oh dear … my chest.
MR WEBB:	Much better! *(They exit, laughing.)*
SAMMY:	*(Checks to see they have gone.)* Cor! At last, something exciting. Wait till I tell Walter! *(He runs out.)*

Scene 8

(Games room. Kids are playing table tennis, card games, darts. They are chatting and socializing. Sammy enters with Walter, who is in full football kit.)

SAMMY:	Let's go over here. *(They move to a corner.)*
WALTER:	What's all this about? I'm supposed to be playing footy.
SAMMY:	Can you keep a secret?
WALTER:	Yeah.

SAMMY: Cross your heart?

WALTER: Cross me heart—

SAMMY: And hope to die.

WALTER: Oh come on, Sammy.

SAMMY: And hope to die.

WALTER: *(Reluctantly.)* An' hope to die. Well?

SAMMY: It's Goldilocks and Spider. They're going to do a bunk. I heard them discussing the whole thing.

WALTER: Never! They wouldn't do that. They're teachers!

SAMMY: I'm telling ya, they're going to pretend to be sick and then skive off to Wales.

WALTER: Get away!

SAMMY: Exciting, eh? A bit of action at last. The best thing that's happened for a long time.

WALTER: *(After a pause.)* Sammy, you're not making this up, are you?

SAMMY: *(Angrily.)* No, I am not! I was sitting outside the staffroom. They opened the window. I heard every word. I even heard the name of the place—Cardigan. *(He produces a map.)* I've looked it up on the map. There!

WALTER: *(Looking.)* Hmmm.

SAMMY: Look, why don't we be detectives and follow them. It'll be a great laugh.

WALTER: No, Sam. You'll only get yourself into trouble.

SAMMY: Chicken …

WALTER: I'm tired of playin' your games, Sam. Look, I'm wanted on the footy field.

SAMMY: You don't believe me, do you? *(Walter is silent.)* You think I've made it all up to get a bit of attention, don't you? *(Walter remains silent.).* Well, go and play your rotten football.

WALTER: Sorry, Sam. *(He runs out.)*

SAMMY: *(Shouting after him.)* You'll see! You'll see!

(The other kids turn and look at Sammy.)

SAMMY: What are you lot gawping at?

(The kids resume their activities. Sammy stomps off in a mood.)

Scene 9

(Cardigan Bay—the hotel veranda.)

MR WEBB: This is the life!

MR BROWN: It is!

MR WEBB: The wide-open spaces …

MR BROWN: Yes …

MR WEBB: Plenty of fresh air.

MR BROWN: It is a bit nippy.

MR WEBB: Nonsense! Blows away the cobwebs.

MR BROWN: Gives you an appetite. What's for lunch?

MR WEBB: Stop thinking about your stomach! Let's go for a walk along the cliffs.

MR BROWN: Again? We've done that twice already. *(Holding his stomach.)* Oooow!

MR WEBB: What's up with you?

MR BROWN: Just a pain in the tum. Ate too much at breakfast.

MR WEBB: Serves you right. *(He laughs.)*

MR BROWN: What's so funny?

MR WEBB: I was just thinking about those poor devils at school.

MR BROWN: Yeah. *(He laughs.)*. What did you tell them?

MR WEBB: Said I'd got a headache—been sick all night.

MR BROWN: I told them an upset stomach. I have one now! Here … you don't think anyone will suspect that—

MR WEBB:	Stop worrying! How could we possibly be found out?
MR BROWN:	I dunno. Somebody might recognize us.
MR WEBB:	But nobody knows us here.
MR BROWN:	You're right. Look, I'm going to have to pay a visit before that walk. Must've been those kippers.
MR WEBB:	Well, hurry up. We haven't got all day.
MR BROWN:	But we have—we're on holiday!
MR WEBB:	Get a move on.

Song: "The Wide-Open Spaces"

(Mr Webb sings.)

> The wide-open spaces,
> The swell of the sea,
> The sound of the sea gulls,
> I'm happy and free.
>
> Oh, this is the life!
> The wind in my hair.
> I feel like a new man.
> I haven't a care.
>
> Oh, I've left my class
> And schoolroom behind,
> And though I am skiving
> I really don't mind.

(He gets increasingly carried away.)

> The sky and the hills,
> The valleys and trees,
> The birds and the fishes,
> Are all friends to me.

(He is joined by sea gulls and other creatures.)

> My heart's on the mountain top,
> My spleen's out of reach,
> My liver and entrails
> Are down on the beach.

> Timetables and textbooks
> Are things of the past,
> But I'm only pretending
> 'Cause I know it can't last.
>
> But as long as I stay here
> I'll be Nature's friend,
> And now my sweet singing
> Has come to an end.

(The sea gulls and creatures vanish. Mr Webb poses dramatically.)

MR BROWN: *(Entering.)* That's better! *(To Mr Webb.)* What's up with you?

MR WEBB: *(Indicating.)* Just looking at those gulls. *(He pulls out his binoculars. Sammy comes into view, wearing a deerstalker, carrying a camera and magnifying glass, very much the amateur sleuth)* Want a look?

MR BROWN: *(Looking through the binoculars and seeing Sammy.)* Aaaaarrggh! It can't be!

MR WEBB: What is it?

MR BROWN: Look … look over there! *(Mr Webb grabs the binoculars.)* What do you see?

MR WEBB: A road … a hedge, a few telegraph poles …

MR BROWN: Nothing else?

MR WEBB: No.

MR BROWN: Thank goodness for that. I could have sworn I saw … *(He laughs.)* No, it's impossible. Let's go for that walk.

(They exit, hotly pursued by Sammy.)

Scene 10

(The dorm.)

CSV: Come on, wake up, you lot! *(The boys start to get up protesting. The CSV moves to Sammy's bed.)* Come on, Sammy. You're on a warning, remember. *(The CSV uncovers pillows where Sammy should be.)* Hey … where's Sammy? *(Boys gather round.)*

1st BOY: Hey look, a note! *(He grabs it.)*

2nd BOY: What's it say?

1st BOY: *(Reading, and then showing them.)* Hello suckers! *(The boys laugh.)*

CSV: Let me see that. *(He snatches the note from 1st Boy and reads.)* Walter, do you know anything about this?

WALTER: What?

2nd BOY: It's Sammy. He's done a runner.

WALTER: Oh, no! The idiot!

CSV: Did he say anything to you? You're his mate.

WALTER: No, he didn't. *(Aside)* Maybe he was telling the truth.

CSV: Are you sure?

WALTER: Yeah, I'm sure. And even if I did know I wouldn't tell you. *(He pauses for effect.)* You don't grass on your mates! *(Cheers from the boys.)*

CSV: Typical! I'd better tell the head. *(He exits.)*

1st BOY: Come on then, Walter. You can tell us.

2nd BOY: Yeah, we're your mates.

WALTER: I'm saying nothing, but I'll tell you this—there's gonna be big trouble! *(He starts to leave.)*

1st BOY: *(Pulling him back.)* Oh, come, don't be a drag. Tell us!

WALTER: All right, then. Who's got the sweets? Come on, get them out. *(Reluctantly the boys produce an assortment of goodies, and Walter pockets them. He addresses the 3rd Boy.)* Where's yours?

3rd BOY: I ain't got none.

WALTER: Well, push off then! *(3rd Boy is bundled out of the way.)*

2nd BOY: Come on then, Wally, let's have it.

CSV: *(Entering.)* Right, you lot, assembly. Now!

WALTER: Sorry, lads. You heard the man. It'll have to keep.

(Walter runs out followed by protesting boys.)

Scene 11

(Large television screen. "Newsflash" displayed.)

NEWSCASTER: We interrupt this programme to bring you a newsflash. The space capsule *Glasnost* carrying Olga and Yuri Androchev—the first couple in space—has run into trouble. Due to technical problems, the capsule will re-enter the Earth's atmosphere earlier than expected. Computer forecasts predict that the capsule will land in the sea west of the British Isles. There is no cause for alarm, but the public is asked to be vigilant. This is the end of the newsflash.

Scene 12

(Cardigan Bay. Mr Webb and Mr Brown are in a rowing boat. Mr Brown is rowing.)

MR WEBB: Aren't you glad we came?

MR BROWN: *(Puffing and panting.)* I'm not so sure.

MR WEBB: The exercise will do you good—work off that enormous lunch. Keep going!

MR BROWN: If I row any harder, me arms'll fall off!

MR WEBB: *(Not listening.)* Eh?

MR BROWN: I said, it's a great laugh, this.

MR WEBB: *(Again not listening.)* Good … good. Well, I think I'll just have forty winks. Make sure we don't run aground now. *(He nods off.)*

MR BROWN: Look at him! Huh, some holiday I've had! A rest? Should've stayed at school. I've had umpteen walks along those cliffs and now this. Honestly! *(He puts on headphones and rows and sings along in time to the music)*

SAMMY: *(Sammy rows on. He's still in his detective gear. He hides behind a rock.)* There they are! Now for some fun. Spider! I say, Spider!

MR WEBB: *(Waking up, disgruntled.)* What do you want?

MR BROWN: *(Removing his headphones.)* Eh?

MR WEBB: What do you want?

MR BROWN: Nothing?

MR WEBB: And stop calling me Spider!

MR BROWN: I didn't.

MR WEBB: Humph! *(He goes back to sleep. Mr Brown replaces his headphones.)*

SAMMY: Could you take my photograph?

MR WEBB: *(To himself.)* Some people! *(To Mr Brown.)* Give me the camera then.

MR BROWN: *(Removing his headphones.)* You what?

MR WEBB: I said, give me the camera then.

MR BROWN: I can't. I left it at the hotel.

MR WEBB: Then how can I take your photograph?

MR BROWN: I don't want you to take my photograph.

MR WEBB: Well, belt up then! Gimme those! *(He snatches the headphones and puts them on.)*

MR BROWN: What's got into you? *(Mr Webb goes back to sleep.)*

SAMMY: Helloooo! Hello, Goldilocks! Over here! *(Mr Brown looks round and sees Sammy, who waves then ducks down.)*

MR BROWN: Aaah! Aaaah! *(He shakes Mr Webb.)* Wake up! wake up! It's terrible! Over there. Over there!

MR WEBB: Look, I'm getting tired of all this—

MR BROWN: Listen … listen! Over there. I saw Johnstone. Sammy Johnstone.

MR WEBB: Sammy Johnstone. *The* Sammy Johnstone? *(Mr Brown nods. Mr Webb then tries to reassure Mr Brown.)* Sammy Johnstone is at school, Sammy Johnstone is miles away.

SAMMY: *(Popping up.)* Oh no he not! Smile please! *(Sammy takes a photograph.)*

MR WEBB: Johnstone! What are you doing here? You should be at school.

SAMMY: You can talk, Spider!

MR WEBB: How dare you! I'm going to telephone the school immediately. *(To Mr Brown.)* Row me back to shore!

MR BROWN: Hang on. We can't do that.

SAMMY: Goldilocks is right. Try talking your way out of this one.

MR WEBB: Johnstone, I'll … I'll—

SAMMY: *You* won't do anything, Spider. *(He taps the camera.)* I've got evidence. You're snookered!

MR BROWN: *(Panicking.)* Evidence! He's got evidence!

MR WEBB: Pull yourself together. He's only bluffing!

SAMMY: Oh yeah? Well just wait till Old Whatisname sees these. *(He taps the camera again.)*

MR BROWN: Old Whatisname?

MR WEBB:	He means the head.
SAMMY:	And I expect the lads'll have a good old hoo-ha as well.
MR BROWN:	I knew we shouldn't have come. I'm ruined. My career is in tatters, and it's all your fault!
MR WEBB:	*My* fault, now just a minute—
SAMMY:	Dry your eyes, Goldilocks. I'm sure we can come to some … arrangement?
MR WEBB:	Eh? That's blackmail.
MR BROWN:	How much do you want Sammy?
MR WEBB:	You're not going to give in to a boy. Now, look here Johnstone—
MR BROWN:	No, you belt up, Spider. The lad only wanted a bit of fun, didn't you, Sammy? *(Sammy nods. Mr Brown addresses Mr Webb again.)* He's letting us off the hook, you nincompoop. *(To Sammy.)* Come on, Sammy, let's go ashore and we'll find a nice café that sells them big ice creams with all the fancy bits sticking out.
SAMMY:	Ooooh, great! You're a pal, Goldilocks!

(Blackout)

Newscaster: (Voice over.) And we've been tracking the capsule since it re-entered the atmosphere. It's sailing down to Earth. Oh, no! It's going to crash land! But wait … the wind's changed. The capsule is heading straight into the bay. Unbelievable! It's unbelievable. The astronauts have escaped certain death. But there's something there. We can't tell what it is. There's going to be a collision. It's … It's … The capsule has come down in Cardigan Bay!

(Towards the end of the Newscaster's speech there is a deafening noise mingled with shouts from Sammy, Mr Brown, and Mr Webb. The lights snap on to reveal a space capsule on which the words "USSR Glasnost" are boldly displayed. The capsule is flanked on one side by Sammy's boat and on the other by Mr Brown and Mr Webb's boat.)

SAMMY: Crikey! A space capsule!

(The door to the capsule creaks and opens Yuri Androchev gets out.)

YURI: *(To Sammy, holding out his hand.)* Hello, I am friend.

SAMMY: *(Taking his hand.)* Amazing!

OLGA: *(From inside the capsule.)* Who is, Yuri?

YURI: Ees little boy.

OLGA: *(Emerging and shaking Sammy's hand.)* 'Allo, little boy. How is you?

SAMMY: Unbelievable!

YURI: *(Noticing Mr Brown and Mr Webb.)* Ees your friends?

(Sammy nods vacantly. Mr Brown and Mr Webb are open mouthed.)

SAMMY: *(To himself.)* Astronauts from space. I dreamt it. No one's gonna believe this!

OLGA: Such nice little boy. Your name, what is?

SAMMY: *(Snapping out of it.)* Eh? Oh … Sammy.

YURI: Hello Sammy. I is Yuri. This Olga.

SAMMY: How do you do, Yuri? Pleased to meet you Olga.

(The Press of the World arrive in a speedboat)

POW: Well come on, then, let's have a photo! *(Sammy lines up with Olga and Yuri.)* Say cheese! *(They smile.)* Thank you! *(To the teachers.)* Come on, you can be in this one.

MR BROWN: *(Panicking.)* Oh, no! We're not here!

POW: Don't you want your picture in the paper?

MR WEBB: *(Also panicking.)* No. No!

POW: Don't be bashful! *(Tries to take photograph.)*

MR WEBB: *(To Mr Brown.)* We'd better get out of here! *(Mr Brown rows off furiously.)*

POW: *(Taking notes.)* How was the trip, Yuri?

YURI: Ees good.

POW: Olga, did you argue much up there?

OLGA: Only when Yuri forget put top on toothpaste tube. Ees good joke, no?

POW: Very good, Olga. *(Turning to Sammy.)* Now, who are you?

SAMMY: I'm Sammy Johnstone.

POW: And where d'you live, Sam?

SAMMY: In a children's home.

POW: What? Don't tell me you're an orphan!

SAMMY: *(Surprised.)* I am, actually.

POW: Brilliant! What a story! They'll love this—*Orphan in Space Welcome*—

SAMMY: *(Quickly catching on.)* There's something else you should know—I dreamt this would happen, but I never really gave it another thought.

POW: *(Scribbling furiously.)* Amazing! *Dream Orphan Welcome for Glasnost Astronauts.* It's a scoop! It's hot! It's a sensation! *(Police siren is heard. The police arrive in a speedboat.)*

POLICE OFFICER: *(Shaking hands.)* Welcome back, Olga, Yuri. Let's get you ashore. *(Sees Sammy.)* Wait a minute, are you Samuel Johnstone?

SAMMY: That's me!

POLICE OFFICER:	Then you're nicked! *(He puts handcuffs on Sammy.)* This boy is a runaway from a children's home. We've been told to keep a look out for 'im.
POW:	Incredible! *Runaway Dream Orphan in Astronaut Welcome Arrested.* What a story! This is my lucky day.
POLICE OFFICER:	You'd better come with me, son. *(Sammy zooms off with the police officer.)*
OLGA:	*(To POW.)* Please excuse—what ees orphan?
Press:	*(Still scribbling.)* Oh, it means he doesn't have a mum or dad.
OLGA:	Oh! You hear, Yuri? *(Yuri nods.)* Ees sad, very sad. 'Bye leetle Sammy.
POW:	Right then, you two, you'd better come back in my boat.
YURI:	Ees kind of you.
POW:	Jump in! *(They get into the boat.)* Now, Olga, you mentioned toothpaste, what actual brand was that?

(They zoom off.)

Allan Sherwood

Music into Song: "Special Feature"

(Kids and staff sing)

>Special feature! Read all about it!
>Sammy Johnstone is hot, hot news.
>He's the boy who met the astronauts.
>He's the boy whose dream came true.
>
>His picture is in every paper,
>His story is on everyone's lips.
>Sammy Johnstone met the astronauts.
>Then the poor wee soul was nicked.
>
>He went back to the children's home,
>A conquering hero to his mates.
>They welcomed him with open arms
>And carried him singing through the gates.

Old Whatisname at first pretended
Not to be impressed,
But he could not conceal his joy
And celebrated with the rest.

Scene 13

(The Children's Home. The boys, Mr Brown, Mr Webb, and the CSV are all assembled. The head is addressing Sammy.)

THE HEAD:	Well, young Sam, I never thought there'd come the day when I would be glad to say that a boy had … absconded, but I'm saying it now—I'm glad! We're world famous. Everybody knows about us now, and it's thanks to you. But, tell me, how did you know where to go? *(Anxious looks from Mr Brown and Mr Webb.)*
SAMMY:	Well … it was like I said—I dreamt it!
MR BROWN:	Yeah. Well done, Sammy.
MR WEBB:	Bravo!
MR BROWN:	*(Aside to Sammy.)* No hard feelings, eh?
SAMMY:	*(Aside to Mr Brown.)* Naaah! Here's that roll of film.
MR BROWN:	Thanks, lad. You're a pal. I'll see you all right.
MR WEBB:	*(As Mr Brown shows him the film.)* That was a close one!
THE HEAD:	And now we have some special visitors to see you, Sammy.

(Olga and Yuri enter still in their astronaut gear. Mr Brown and Mr Webb are horror struck.)

SAMMY: *(Going to them.)* Olga, Yuri.

OLGA: Hallo, leetle Sammy.

YURI: How is you, junior?

SAMMY: Couldn't be better.

OLGA: I have something to say, and I want you all listen. Come here, leetle Sam. *(Sammy moves to Olga.)* All day, every day for many years Yuri and I we dream of having leetle boy to call our own, but no babies come. You understand?

YURI: Ees bad luck, no? But you young Sammy is answer to our prayers.

OLGA: We think ees miracle that you meet us when we come out capsule.

YURI: What Olga try to say is that we want you be our own leetle boy.

SAMMY: You mean you're going to be my mum and dad?

OLGA: If you like.

SAMMY: Yes, please! *(Olga, Sammy, and Yuri hug.)*

YURI:	*(To head.)* Ees settle then? *(Head nods. Yuri recognizes Mr Brown and Mr Webb.)* 'Allo, how ees you? Look, Olga, ees Sammy's friends.
OLGA:	*(Beaming at Mr Brown and Mr Webb.)* Hallo again! *(The head starts to get interested, and the boys sense trouble.)*
MR WEBB:	*(To Olga.)* Sorry do I know you?
OLGA:	You is funny man. Big joker. Ha, ha, no?
YURI:	*(Innocently to the head.)* When we comes out capsule who we see with leetle Sam but these two mens.
THE HEAD:	*(To Mr Webb.)* Is this true?
MR WEBB:	*(Gulping.)* There must be some mistake.
YURI:	*(Producing a photograph.)* No mistake, boss man. Here is photo which press man take of us. These two mens are here at back. See?
THE HEAD:	Let me see that. *(Yuri gives the photograph to the head. As he looks his anger starts to build.)* So … headaches, is it? Pains in the tum, eh? I'll give you both a pain in the backside!
MR BROWN:	Wait! No!
MR WEBB:	*(Simultaneously with Mr Brown.)* We can explain! Help! *(They run off chased by the head.)*
SAMMY:	*(Shouting after them.)* Sorry, lads!

Allan Sherwood

YURI: Ha, ha. Ees funny man, your boss! Now we go to our house in Welsh Valley and have beeg, beeg party. Everyones is most welcome!

Music, dance, and celebration

(During the celebration, Mr Brown and Mr Webb appear being chased by the head. The newspaper headlines "The Runaway Comes Home",

"One Beeg Happy Family", "Another Dream Comes True for Sam",

"Sammy Leaves Home for Good" appear in the throng. The dance and celebrations continue to end.)

About the Illustrator

Lucy Venables is an 18 year old student with a passion for Art and Harry Potter.

Lucy has been a keen artist from a very young age when she discovered finger paints, wax crayons and then felt-tip pens. Currently studying Health and Social Care at South Cheshire College, Lucy has been offered a place to study Psychology at Liverpool John Moores University but continues to draw in the majority of her spare time.

Lucy's inspiration comes from her love of the Harry Potter novels; surrounded by the books, screenplays, films and memorabilia, Lucy draws using thick, oil-based lead pencils and acid-free 150 gsm paper.

Lucy was invited to illustrate "These Kids" after Allan viewed examples of her work.

Using her unique style, Lucy will take you on a journey through residential care and help bring Allan's words to life.

Lightning Source UK Ltd.
Milton Keynes UK
UKHW01f2026310518
323540UK00001B/28/P